My Lutheran Notebook

Hymns, Quotes, and Prayers for Inspiration

CONCORDIA PUBLISHING HOUSE • SAINT LOUIS

Copyright © 2021 Concordia Publishing House
3558 S. Jefferson Ave., St. Louis, MO 63118-3968
1-800-325-3040 • cph.org

All rights reserved. No part of this publication may be reproduced, stored in a retrieval system, or transmitted, in any form or by any means, electronic, mechanical, photocopying, recording, or otherwise, without the prior written permission of Concordia Publishing House.

Scripture quotations are from the ESV® Bible (The Holy Bible, English Standard Version®), copyright © 2001 by Crossway, a publishing ministry of Good News Publishers. Used by permission. All rights reserved.

Quotations marked SC taken from *Luther's Small Catechism with Explanation*, copyright © 1986, 2017 Concordia Publishing House. All rights reserved.

Quotations marked *LSB* taken from *Lutheran Service Book,* copyright © 2006 Concordia Publishing House. All rights Reserved.

Quotations marked WLS taken from *What Luther Says,* copyright © 1959 Concordia Publishing House. All rights reserved.

Quotations marked AE are from Martin Luther. *Luther's Works: American Edition.* General editors: Jaroslav Pelikan, Helmut T. Lehmann, Christopher Boyd Brown, and Benjamin T. G. Mayes. 82 vols. St. Louis: Concordia, and Philadelphia: Muhlenberg and Fortress, 1955–.

Quotations marked LC taken from *Luther's Large Catechism* in *Concordia: The Lutheran Confessions,* second edition, copyright © 2006 Concordia Publishing House. All rights reserved.

Quotations marked *TLSB* taken from *The Lutheran Study Bible,* copyright © 2009 Concordia Publishing House. All rights reserved.

Manufactured in China

1 2 3 4 5 6 7 8 9 10   30 29 28 27 26 25 24 23 22 21

I praise You, for I am fearfully and wonderfully made.
Wonderful are Your works; my soul knows it very well.

(Psalm 139:14)

Praise God, from whom all blessings flow.
(*LSB* 805:1)

Guard my first springs of thought and will And with Thyself my spirit fill.
(*LSB* 868:4)

Jesus, in Your name begun Be the day's endeavor;
Grant that it may well be done To Your praise forever.
(*LSB* 869:5)

I believe that God . . . richly and daily provides me with all that I need to support this body and life.
(SC, Explanation of the First Article)

I leave all things to God's direction; He loves me both in joy and woe.
His will is good, sure His affection; His tender love is true, I know.
My fortress and my rock is He: What pleases God, that pleases me.
(*LSB* 719:1)

I am trusting Thee to guide me; Thou alone shalt lead,
Ev'ry day and hour supplying All my need.
(*LSB* 729:4)

Rejoice in hope, be patient in tribulation, be constant in prayer.
(Romans 12:12)

You should not imagine that the life of a Christian is something stationary and inactive. On the contrary, it is a transition and a progress from vices to virtues, from brightness to brightness, from goodness to goodness.
(WLS § 698)

Heavenly Father, in whom we live and move and have our being, we humbly pray You so to guide and govern us by Your Word and Spirit, that in all the cares and occupations of our life we may not forget You but remember that we are ever walking in Your sight; through Jesus Christ, our Lord.
(*LSB,* p. 284)

Your Word inspires my heart within;
Your Word grants healing from my sin;
Your Word has pow'r to guide and bless;
Your Word brings peace and happiness.

(*LSB* 908:2)

Glad my eyes, and warm my heart.
(*LSB* 873:2)

Blessed Jesus, Blessed Jesus, Hear us children when we pray.
LSB 711:2)

O Comforter of priceless worth, Send peace and unity on earth.
(*LSB* 655:3)

Lord of harvest, great and kind, Rouse to action heart and mind;
Let the gath'ring nations all See Your light and heed Your call.
(*LSB* 830:4)

Since He is ours, We fear no powers, Not of earth nor sin or death.
(*LSB* 818:2)

Before the ending of the day, Creator of the world, we pray!
Thy grace and peace to us allow And be our guard and keeper now.
(*LSB* 889:1)

My soul and body keep from harm, And over all extend Your arm.
(*LSB* 876:2)

As You, Lord, have lived for others, So may we for others live.
(*LSB* 842:2)

Grace hears, it leads, it drives, it draws, it changes, it works all in man, and lets itself be distinctly felt and experienced. It is hidden, but its works are evident. Words and works show where it dwells, just as the fruit and the leaves of a tree indicate the kind and the character of the tree.
(WLS § 1877)

God placed His church in the midst of the world, among countless external activities and callings, not in order that Christians should become monks but so that they may live in fellowship and that our works and the exercises of our faith may become known among men.
(AE 54:307)

Rejoice always, pray without ceasing, give thanks in all circumstances; for this is the will of God in Christ Jesus for you.

(1 Thessalonians 5:16–18)

Let each day begin with prayer, Praise, and adoration.
(*LSB* 869:2)

All my blessings come from Thee; Oh, how good Thou art to me!
(*LSB* 887:4)

We give Thee but Thine own, Whate'er the gift may be;
All that we have is Thine alone, A trust, O Lord from Thee.
(*LSB* 781:1)

Thy praise shall sound from shore to shore
Till suns shall rise and set no more. Alleluia!
(*LSB* 816:2)

By Thee are given The gifts of heaven,
Thou the true Redeemer art.

(*LSB* 818:1)

Almighty God, all that we possess is from Your loving hand. Give us grace that we may honor You with all we own, always remembering the account we must one day give to Jesus Christ, our Lord.

(*LSB*, p. 311)

He lives and grants me daily breath.

(*LSB* 461:7)

I am weak, but Thou art mighty; Hold me with Thy pow'rful hand.
(*LSB* 918:1)

My hope is built on nothing less Than Jesus' blood and righteousness;
No merit of my own I claim But wholly lean on Jesus' name.
On Christ, the solid rock, I stand; All other ground is sinking sand.
(*LSB* 575:1)

The Lord, my God be praised, My trust, my life from heaven.
(*LSB* 794:2)

Unite all those who walk apart; Confirm the weak and doubting heart.

(*LSB* 839:4)

The Lord our God is good: His mercy is forever sure.
(*LSB* 791:4)

Ponder anew What the Almighty can do As with His love He befriends you.
(*LSB* 790:4)

If you believe, then it is impossible that your heart will not laugh for joy in God, and become free, sure, and courageous. . . . Therefore, your love breaks forth and does for everyone whatever it can, preaches and proclaims the truth wherever it can, and rejects everything which is not preached or lived according to this doctrine.

(AE 75:233, 234)

We neither should nor want to know what God does not want to reveal to us; we let it pass and permit *Him* take care of it.

(WLS § 3739)

Who will answer, gladly saying, "Here am I, send me, send me"?
(*LSB* 826:1)

Though all the world forsake His Word,
I and my house will serve the Lord!

(*LSB* 862:5)

This is the day the Lord has made; He calls the hours His own.
(*LSB* 903:1)

I am trusting Thee, Lord Jesus; Never let me fall.
I am trusting Thee forever And for all.

(*LSB* 729:6)

Lord, on You I cast my burden—Sink it in the deepest sea!
Let me know Your gracious pardon, Cleanse me from iniquity.
Let Your Spirit leave me never; Make me only Yours forever.
(*LSB* 608:4)

But they who wait for the Lord shall renew their strength; they shall mount up with wings like eagles; they shall run and not be weary; they shall walk and not faint.

(Isaiah 40:31)

Order my footsteps by The Word And make my heart sincere;
Let sin have no dominion, Lord, But keep my conscience clear.
(*LSB* 707:2)

Order my goings, Direct all my doings; As it may please Thee,
Retain or release me; all I commit to Thy fatherly hand.
(*LSB* 726:2)

Forgive me, Lord, where I have erred By loveless act and thoughtless word.
(*LSB* 844:3)

Heal our wrongs and help our need.
(*LSB* 842:1)

Lord, how shall I thank Thee rightly?
I acknowledge that by Thee I am saved eternally.
Let me not forget it lightly, But to Thee at all times cleave
And my heart true peace receive.
(*LSB* 897:3)

Teach me to live that I may dread The grave as little as my bed.
Teach me to die that so I may Rise glorious at the awe-full day.
(*LSB* 883:3)

Jesus, Savior, wash away All that has been wrong today;
Help me ev'ry day to be Good and gentle, more like Thee.
(*LSB* 887:2)

Thou knowest all my griefs and fears, Thy grace abused, my misspent years;
Yet now to Thee with contrite tears, Christ crucified, I come.
(*LSB* 560:2)

When the devil comes and would also have a share in you, and hell would devour you, direct them to Christ; then you will silence them.
(WLS § 590)

Preserve me, O God, for in You I take refuge.

(Psalm 16:1)

Forth in Thy name, O Lord, I go, My daily labor to pursue,
Thee, only Thee, resolved to know In all I think or speak or do.
(*LSB* 854:1)

We blossom and flourish as leaves on the tree
And wither and perish—but naught changes Thee.
(*LSB* 802:3)

Take my will and make it Thine, It shall be no longer mine;
Take my heart, it is Thine own, It shall be Thy royal throne.
(*LSB* 783:5)

Therefore do not be anxious about tomorrow, for tomorrow will be anxious for itself. Sufficient for the day is its own trouble.
(Matthew 6:34)

What can be more pleasing to God and more useful for people than to live in your calling so that God receives honor and with your example to lead others to love God's Word and praise His name?

(AE 79:148)

With the Lord begin your task; Jesus will direct it.
For His aid and counsel ask; Jesus will perfect it.
(*LSB* 869:1)

Give, and it will be given to you. Good measure, pressed down, shaken together, running over, will be put into your lap. For with the measure you use it will be measured back to you.

(Luke 6:38)

Look at the birds of the air: they neither sow nor reap nor gather into barns, and yet your heavenly Father feeds them. Are you not of more value than they?
(Matthew 6:26)

All that I am and love most dearly—Receive it all, O Lord, from me.
Let me confess my faith sincerely; Help me Your faithful child to be!
Let nothing that I am or own Serve any will but Yours alone.
(*LSB* 590:4)

Though a thousand other duties and relationships may cry out to you, remember that this one relationship—to Christ—has the highest priority. Like the beloved disciple, lean on the Lord and bring your requests to Him. He will hear your pleas and answer you with loving-kindness. Though a thousand other duties and relationships may cry out to Him, He will always have time for you.
(*TLSB*, p. 1780)

Jesus, Savior, pilot me Over life's tempestuous sea;
Unknown waves before me roll, Hiding rock and treach'rous shoal.
Chart and compass come from Thee. Jesus, Savior, pilot me.
(*LSB* 715:1)

Lord God, You have called Your servants to ventures of which we cannot see the ending, by paths as yet untrodden, through perils unknown. Give us faith to go out with good courage, not knowing where we go but only that Your hand is leading us and Your love supporting us; through Jesus Christ, our Lord.
(*LSB*, p. 311)

So we fell under God's wrath and displeasure and were doomed to eternal damnation, just as we had merited and deserved. There was no counsel, help, or comfort until this only and eternal Son of God—in His immeasurable goodness—had compassion upon our misery and wretchedness. He came from heaven to help us [John 1:9].

(LC Part 2, paragraphs 28–29)

Ev'ry morn with Jesus rise, And when the day is ended,
In His name then close your eyes; Be to Him commended.
(*LSB* 869:1)

Goodness and mercy all my life Shall surely follow me;
And in God's house forever more My dwelling place shall be.
(*LSB* 710:5)

We pray that He would deal graciously with us and forgive, as He has promised, and so grant us a joyful and confident conscience to stand before Him in prayer.
(LC, Part 3, paragraph 92)

Take my will and make it Thine, It shall be no longer mine;
Take my heart, it is Thine own, It shall be Thy royal throne.
(*LSB* 783:5)

Reason sees the world as extremely ungodly, and therefore it murmurs. The Spirit sees nothing but God's benefits in the world and therefore begins to sing.
(AE 17:356)

Break down the wall that would divide Thy children, Lord, on every side.
(*LSB* 844:2)

Guard Thou the lips from sin, the hearts from shame,
That in this house have called upon Thy name.
(*LSB* 917:2)

Stay with us, till day is done: No tears nor dark shall dim the sun.
Cheer the heart, Your grace impart: Jesus, bring eternal life.
(*LSB* 879:5)

Though you have not seen Him, you love Him. Though you do not now see Him, you believe in Him and rejoice with joy that is inexpressible and filled with glory, obtaining the outcome of your faith, the salvation of your souls.

(1 Peter 1:8–9)

Though sin bite, death terrify, and the devil let himself be felt in temptation, these are, after all, clouds; the heaven of grace rules and wins out.
(WLS § 712)

Grant us wisdom, grant us courage For the facing of this hour.
(*LSB* 850:1)

God is my comfort and my trust, My hope and life abiding;
And to His counsel, wise and just, I yield, in Him confiding.
(*LSB* 758:2)

May Your angel guards defend us, Slumber sweet Your mercy send us,
Holy dreams and hopes attend us All through the night.
(*LSB* 877:1)

If we firmly held God to be the Creator, we should certainly believe that He has in His hands heaven and earth and everything they contain. Even more: If we were to see the shattered globe sink to ruin with all the elements and threaten our necks, we should nevertheless say: Even though you fall, you will not fall unless God wills it.
(WLS § 693)

I believe in one God, the Father Almighty, maker of heaven and earth and of all things visible and invisible.
(*LSB*, Nicene Creed, Article 1)

Throughout life a faithful friend is a very great blessing and a very precious treasure.

(WLS § 1588)

What a friend we have in Jesus, All our sins and griefs to bear! What a privilege to carry Everything to God in prayer.
(*LSB* 770:1)

Let my near and dear ones be Always near and dear to Thee;
O bring me and all I love To Thy happy home above.
(*LSB* 887:3)

He never shall forsake His flock, His chosen generation;
He is their refuge and their rock, Their peace and their salvation.
(*LSB* 819:4)

Holy, holy, holy! Lord God Almighty!
All Thy works shall praise Thy name
in earth and sky and sea.
(*LSB* 507:4)

O Lord, open my lips, and my mouth will declare Your praise.
(Psalm 51:15)

What is important for a good prayer is not many words, as Christ says in Matthew 6:7, but rather a turning to God frequently and with heartfelt longing, and doing so without ceasing [1 Thessalonians 5:17].

(AE 43:12)

I thank You, my heavenly Father, through Jesus Christ, Your dear Son, that You have kept me this night from all harm and danger; and I pray that You would keep me this day also from sin and every evil, that all my doings and life may please You. For into Your hands I commend myself, my body and soul, and all things. Let Your holy angel be with me, that the evil foe may have no power over me.
(SC, Luther's Morning Prayer)

Praise the Almighty, my soul, adore Him! Yes, I will laud Him until death; with songs and anthems I come before Him As long as He allows me breath. From Him my life and all things came; Bless, O my soul, His holy name. Alleluia, alleluia!
(*LSB* 797:1)

You only dearest Lord, My soul's delight shall be;
You are my peace, my rest. What is the world to me!
(*LSB* 730:1)

All coldness from my heart remove; My ev'ry act, word, thought be love.
(*LSB* 683:2)

You should be certain that angels are protecting you when you go to sleep, yea, that they are protecting you also in all your business, whether you enter your home or leave your home.
(WLS § 70)

Where there is a drop of evil, there is also a veritable sea of God's benefactions. For in reality all evil is very small; and the little cross we bear is a trifle if we compare it with the benefits that come to us from creation, redemption, and sanctification. Moreover, in the future life these blessings will be still more splendid.
(WLS § 23)

Great are the works of the Lord, studied by all who delight in them. Full of splendor and majesty is His work, and His righteousness endures forever.
(Psalm 111:2–3)

We give our minds to understand Your ways;
Hands, eyes, and voice to serve Your great design.
(*LSB* 786:2)

May God the Father, God the Son, God the Spirit bless us! Let all the world praise Him alone, Let solemn awe possess us. Now let our hearts say, "Amen!"
(*LSB* 823:3)

I will give you the keys of the kingdom of heaven, and whatever you bind on earth shall be bound in heaven, and whatever you loose on earth shall be loosed in heaven.

(Matthew 16:19)

If you forgive the sins of any, they are forgiven them; if you withhold forgiveness from any, it is withheld.
(John 20:23)

Just as I am, though tossed about With many a conflict, many a doubt, Fightings and fears within, without, O Lamb of God, I come, I come. (*LSB* 570:3)

Thine forever, Lord of Life! Shield us through our earthly strife.
Thou, the life, the truth, the way, Guide us to the realms of day.
(*LSB* 687:3)

I know very well that I do not have a single work which is pure; but surely I am baptized, and through my Baptism God, who cannot lie, has bound Himself not to count my sin against me but to slay it and blot it out.
(WLS § 161)

Come, Thou Fount of ev'ry blessing, Tune my heart to sing Thy grace; Streams of mercy, never ceasing, Call for songs of loudest praise. While the hope of endless glory Fills my heart with joy and love, Teach me ever to adore Thee; May I still Thy goodness prove.
(*LSB* 686:1)

Create in me a new heart, Lord, That gladly I obey Your Word.
Let what You will be my desire, And with new life my soul inspire.
(*LSB* 704:3)

Direct, control, suggest this day All I design or do or say
That all my pow'rs with all their might In Thy sole glory may unite.
(*LSB* 868:5)

Grant us Your Holy Spirit that we may forsake all covetous desires and the inordinate love of riches. Deliver us from the pursuit of passing things that we may seek the kingdom of Your Son and trust in His righteousness and so find blessedness and peace; through Jesus Christ, our Lord.
(*LSB*, p. 311)

By grace I'm saved, grace free and boundless;
My soul, believe and doubt it not.
(*LSB* 566:1)

Fill with the radiance of Your grace The souls now lost in error's maze.
(*LSB* 839:2)

I do not merit favor, Lord, My weight of sin would break me;
In all my guilty heart's discord, O Lord, do not forsake me.
In my distress this comforts me That You receive me graciously,
O Christ, my Lord of mercy!

(*LSB* 625:4)

Thy mercies, how tender, how firm to the end, Our maker, defender, redeemer, and friend!

(*LSB* 804:5)

Take the task He gives you gladly, Let His work your pleasure be;
Answer quickly when He calleth, "Here am I, send me, send me!"
(*LSB* 826:4)

You see how rich a Christian, or one who is baptized, really is. Even if he so desired, he is unable to lose his salvation, however much he sins, unless he refuses to believe; for no sins except unbelief alone can condemn him.
(WLS § 162)

Enlighten those whose inmost minds Some dark delusion haunts and blinds.
(*LSB* 839:2)

Then let us follow Christ, our Lord, And take the cross appointed And, firmly clinging to His Word, In suff'ring be undaunted. For those who bear the battle's strain The crown of heav'nly life obtain.

(*LSB* 688:5)

Beautiful Savior, Lord of the nations, Son of God and Son of Man!
Glory and honor, Praise, adoration Now and forevermore be Thine!
(*LSB* 537:4)

Let me be Thine forever, My faithful God and Lord; Let me forsake Thee never Nor wander from Thy Word.
Lord, do not let me waver, But give me steadfastness,
And for such grace forever Thy holy name I'll bless.
(*LSB* 689:1)

Teach us the lesson Thou has taught: To feel for those Thy blood hath bought,
That ev'ry word and deed and thought May work a work for Thee.
(*LSB* 852:3)

Think of the Scriptures as the loftiest and noblest of holy things, as the richest of mines which can never be sufficiently explored, in order that you may find that divine wisdom which God here lays before you in such simple guise as to quench all pride.
(AE 35:236)

The Word is so effective that whenever it is seriously contemplated, heard, and used, it is bound never to be without fruit [Isaiah 55:11, Mark 4:20]. It always awakens new understanding, pleasure, and devoutness and produces a pure heart and pure thoughts [Philippians 4:8].
(LC, Part 1, paragraph 101)

God will not give you His Spirit without the external Word; so take your cue from that. His command to write, preach, read, hear, sing, speak, etc., outwardly was not given in vain.

(AE 34:286)

You have multiplied, O LORD my God, Your wondrous deeds
and Your thoughts toward us; none can compare with You!
I will proclaim and tell of them, yet they are more than can be told.
(Psalm 40:5)

How sweet the name of Jesus sounds In a believer's ear!
It soothes our sorrows, heals our wounds, And drives away our fear.
(*LSB* 524:1)

Intercessor, Friend of sinners, Earth's Redeemer, hear our plea.

(*LSB* 821:3)

I walk with angels all the way, They shield me and befriend me;
All Satan's pow'r is held at bay When heav'nly hosts attend me.
(*LSB* 716:4)

We pray You, O Lord, to keep our tongues from evil and our lips from speaking deceit, that as Your holy angels continuously sing praises to You in heaven, so may we at all times glorify You on earth; through Jesus Christ, our Lord.
(*LSB*, p. 312)

My God has all things in His keeping; He is the ever faithful friend.
He gives me laughter after weeping, And all His ways in blessings end.
His love endures eternally: what pleases God, that pleases me.
(*LSB* 719:4)

Now that the daylight fills the sky, We lift our hearts to God on high,
That He, in all we do or say, Would keep us free from harm today.
(*LSB* 870:1)

I need Thy presence ev'ry passing hour;
What but Thy grace can foil the tempter's pow'r?
Who like Thyself my guide and stay can be?
Through cloud and sunshine, O abide with me.
(*LSB* 878:2)

Fear not, for I am with you; be not dismayed, for I am your God; I will strengthen you, I will help you, I will uphold you with My righteous right hand.

(Isaiah 41:10)

His strength within my weakness Will make me bold to say
How His redeeming power Transforms my stubborn clay.
(*LSB* 835:3)

Repent therefore, and turn back, that your sins may be blotted out, that times of refreshing may come from the presence of the Lord, and that He may send the Christ appointed for you, Jesus.
(Acts 3:19–20)

The Lord has promised good to me, His Word my hope secures.
(*LSB* 744:2)

Create in me a clean heart, O God, and renew a right spirit within me. Cast me not away from Thy presence, and take not Thy Holy Spirit from me. Restore unto me the joy of Thy salvation, and uphold me with Thy free spirit. Amen.

(*LSB*, pp. 192–93)

Christians must suffer very much because the devil and the whole world are bitterly hostile to them. . . . How are they able to bear all these things and be patient besides? Only by continuing to cling to the Word and saying: Let things go as they go; I am not of this world but of God.

(WLS § 721)

I have said these things to you, that in Me you may have peace.
In the world you will have tribulation. But take heart;
I have overcome the world.

(John 16:33)

Restore and quicken, soothe and bless, With Your life-giving breath.
To hands that work and eyes that see Give wisdom's healing pow'r
That whole and sick and weak and strong May praise You ever more.
(*LSB* 846:3)

When in the night I sleepless lie, My soul with heav'nly thoughts supply;
Let no ill dreams disturb my rest, No pow'rs of darkness me molest.
(*LSB* 883:5)

All holy Lord, in humble prayer We ask tonight Thy watchful care.
O grant us calm repose in Thee, A quiet night, from perils free.
(*LSB* 882:2)

I thank You, my heavenly Father, through Jesus Christ, Your dear Son, that You have graciously kept me this day; and I pray that You would forgive me all my sins where I have done wrong, and graciously keep me this night. For into Your hands I commend myself, my body and soul, and all things. Let Your holy angel be with me, that the evil foe may have no power over me. Amen.

(SC, Luther's Evening Prayer)

In sickness, sorrow, want, or care, May we each other's burdens share; May we, where help is needed, there Give help as unto Thee!
(*LSB* 852:5)

Hush the storm of strife and passion, Bid its cruel discords cease.

(*LSB* 842:3)

Keep me from saying words That later need recalling;
Guard me lest idle speech May from my lips be falling;
But when within my place I must and ought to speak,
Then to my words give grace Lest I offend the weak.
(*LSB* 696:3)

We are still sinful and spiritually weak. Therefore [Christ] must unceasingly represent us before the Father and intercede for us that such weakness and sin may not be reckoned to our account. Rather He must grant us the strength and power of the Holy Spirit to overcome sin.
(WLS § 551)

You are the God who works wonders; You have made known
Your might among the peoples.
(Psalm 78:14)

God's first act, the creation, is an act of grace. God acts freely to reflect His character, making the world "very good" (Genesis 1:31). Even after the fall and the coming of sin, much of the goodness that God built into creation remains.
(*TLSB*, note on Genesis 1:1, p. 12)

Whatever God does not tell you, or does not want to tell you, you should not desire to know. And you should honor Him enough to believe that He sees that it is not necessary, useful, or good for you to know.

(WLS § 209)

When I was a child, I spoke like a child, I thought like a child, I reasoned like a child. When I became a man, I gave up childish ways. For now we see in a mirror dimly, but then face to face. Now I know in part; then I shall know fully, even as I have been fully known. So now faith, hope, and love abide, these three; but the greatest of these is love.

(1 Corinthians 13:11–13)

For God, who said, "Let light shine out of darkness," has shone in our hearts to give the light of the knowledge of the glory of God in the face of Jesus Christ.
(2 Corinthians 4:6)

Melt the clouds of sin and sadness, Drive the gloom of doubt away.
(*LSB* 803:1)

Let no one imagine that we who are Christians shall have peace on earth or get rid of our enemies. On the contrary, we should cheerfully prepare ourselves and expect enemies one after another without fail to attack and persecute Christendom until the Last Day.
(WLS § 605)

Praise Him for His grace and favor To His people in distress.
(*LSB* 793:2)

Lord Jesus, since You love me, Now spread
Your wings above me And shield me from alarm.
Though Satan would devour me, Let angel guards sing o'er me:
This child of God shall meet no harm.

(*LSB* 880:4)

A Christian is a bold, blessed person, one who pays no attention to the devil or to any misfortune; for he knows that through Christ he is lord over all such matters.
(WLS § 690)

The Lord, my God, be praised, My light, my life from heaven.
(*LSB* 794:1)

O God, give us times of refreshment and peace in the course of this busy life. Grant that we may so use our leisure to rebuild our bodies and renew our minds that we may be opened to the goodness of Your creation; through Jesus Christ, our Lord. (*LSB*, p. 311)

The Bible is a remarkable fountain: the more one draws and drinks of it, the more it stimulates thirst.

(WLS § 196)

"Whoever drinks of the water that I will give him will never be thirsty again. The water that I will give him will become in him a spring of water welling up to eternal life."
(John 4:14)

The true, supreme, and best blessing, in which one can and should really and truly sense the goodness of God, is not temporal possessions but the eternal blessing that God has called us to His holy Gospel.

(WLS § 4012)